TIME FOR KIDS

Workers

Dona Herweck Rice

Consultant

Timothy Rasinski, Ph.D
Kent State University

Publishing Credits

Dona Herweck Rice, *Editor-in-Chief*
Lee Aucoin, *Creative Director*
Conni Medina, M.A.Ed., *Editorial Director*
Jamey Acosta, *Editor*
Robin Erickson, *Designer*
Stephanie Reid, *Photo Editor*
Rachelle Cracchiolo, M.S.Ed., *Publisher*

Image Credits
Cover stefanolunardi/Shutterstock; p.3 DianaLundin/istockphoto; p.4 Photolibrary; p.5 stockstudioX/istockphoto; p.6 auremar/Shutterstock; p.7 ARENA Creative/Shutterstock p.8 Iofoto/Dreamstime; p.9 Monkeybusiness/Dreamstime; p.10 Photolibrary; p.11 pixdeluxe/istockphoto; back cover auremar/Shutterstock

Based on writing from *TIME For Kids.*

TIME For Kids and the *TIME For Kids* logo are registered trademarks of TIME Inc. Used under license.

Teacher Created Materials
5301 Oceanus Drive
Huntington Beach, CA 92649-1030
http://www.tcmpub.com

ISBN 978-1-4333-3572-3

Printed in China WAI002

I work.

I work.

I bring mail.

I work.

I get rid of trash.

I work.

I fix wires.

I work.

I help sick animals.

I work.

I teach children.

I work.
I fight fires.

I work.

I keep you safe.

Many people work.

Words to Know

animals
bring
children
fight
fires
fix
get
help
I
keep
mail
many
of
people
rid
safe
sick
teach
trash
wires
work
you